DISCOVER!

PEOPLE of the PAST

WHO WAS SACAGAWEA?

Robert Clore

Enslow PUBLISHING

Please visit our website, www.enslow.com. For a free color catalog of all our high-quality books, call toll free 1-800-398-2504 or fax 1-877-980-4454.

Cataloging-in-Publication Data
Names: Clore, Robert.
Title: Who was Sacagawea? / Robert Clore.
Description: Buffalo, NY : Enslow Publishing, 2027. | Series: People of the past | Includes glossary.
Identifiers: ISBN 9781978550568 (pbk.) | ISBN 9781978550575 (library bound) | ISBN 9781978550582 (ebook)
Subjects: LCSH: Sacagawea–Juvenile literature. | Lewis and Clark Expedition (1804-1806)–Juvenile literature. | Shoshoni women–Biography–Juvenile literature. | Shoshoni Indians–Biography–Juvenile literature.
Classification: LCC F592.7.S123 C657 2027 | DDC 978.0049745740092 B–dc23

Published in 2027 by
Enslow Publishing
2544 Clinton Street
Buffalo, NY 14224

Designer: Claire Vanden Branden
Editor: Max Pritchard

Photo Credits: Cover, pp. 1, 9 Wikimedia Commons; p. 5 National Park Service; p. 7 National Archives; p. 11 Library of Congress; p. 13 Humanities Texas; p. 15 Wichakorn Kitrungrot/Shutterstock.com; p. 17 Everett Collection/Shutterstock.com; p. 19 Ace Diamond/Shutterstock.com; p. 21 Frank L. Junior/Shutterstock.com.

Printed in China

CPSIA compliance information: Batch #QS27ENS: For further information contact Enslow Publishing, at 1-800-398-2504.

CONTENTS

BOLDFACE WORDS APPEAR IN THE GLOSSARY.

A FAMOUS GUIDE

Sacagawea was a Native American woman born in the late 1700s. She is famous for helping Meriwether Lewis and William Clark **explore** the western United States.

EARLY LIFE

Some historians believe Sacagawea was born to the Shoshone **tribe** and taken by the Hidatsa tribe at 12 years old. Some Native American historians argue she was always a member of the Hidatsa tribe.

A HIDATSA WINTER VILLAGE

GOING WEST

The Hidatsa tribe sold Sacagawea to fur trader Toussaint Charbonneau in 1804. He bought her as a second wife. He was hired to **interpret** for American explorers Meriwether Lewis and William Clark.

MERIWETHER LEWIS, RIGHT, AND WILLIAM CLARK

Lewis and Clark were studying Western North America. The United States had just bought a large area of land from France. Many Native American tribes lived on this land. Sacagawea was chosen to travel with Lewis and Clark, too. Charbonneau claimed she could speak to the Shoshone for them.

A SHOSHONE ENCAMPMENT, 1870

A HELPFUL GUIDE

Sacagawea had a baby son just before leaving with the explorers in 1805. Together, they were very helpful. Traveling with a woman and baby showed that the explorers did not want to fight.

THE TRAVELERS MEET A NATIVE AMERICAN GROUP.

Sacagawea helped the explorers cross the Rocky Mountains. She knew the best route. She got them horses and a guide from a man who may have been her brother. He was the chief of a nearby Shoshone tribe.

THE ROCKY MOUNTAINS

Sacagawea knew a lot about the land the group traveled through. She found plants that could be eaten. She also made clothing. She was brave and quick during difficult moments. Once, she saved important equipment from a rushing river.

AFTER THE TRAVELS

Some people say Sacagawea died around 1812. However, members of the Hidatsa tribe have provided evidence that she returned to her tribe and lived until 1884. **DNA** tests and tribal histories suggest she had three more children. These tests suggest some modern Hidatsa people are her **descendants**.

SACAGAWEA AND HER FIRST SON, JEAN-BAPTISTE

REMEMBERING SACAGAWEA

There are many places around the United States that honor Sacagawea. A lake, a mountain, a river, and more have been named for her. In 2000, the US **Mint** put her picture on the dollar coin.

LIBERTY
IN GOD
WE TRUST

GLOSSARY

descendants: People who are related to a person who lived in the past.

DNA: Information in the body's cells that helps make people who they are.

explore: To search in order to find out new things.

interpret: To translate from one language to another.

mint: A place where coins are made.

tribe: A group of people who live, work, and move about together.

FOR MORE INFORMATION

Books

Manning, Mick. *Women Who Led the Way*. Hereford, UK: Otter-Barry Books, 2022.

Teton, Randy'L He-Dow. *It's Her Story: Sacajawea*. Chicago, IL: OTTN Pheonix International Publications, 2023.

Websites

Britannica Kids: The Louisiana Purchase
kids.britannica.com/kids/article/Louisiana-Purchase/353399
Learn about the deal that led to Lewis and Clark's journey.

National Geographic Kids: Lewis and Clark
kids.nationalgeographic.com/history/article/lewis-and-clark
Learn more about the journey of Lewis and Clark.

INDEX